The
U.S. Supreme Court

by Patricia J. Murphy

Content Adviser: Kathleen M. Kendrick, Project Historian,
National Museum of American History, Smithsonian Institution

Social Science Adviser: Professor Sherry L. Field,
Department of Curriculum and Instruction,
College of Education, The University of Texas at Austin

Reading Adviser: Dr. Linda D. Labbo, Department of Reading Education,
College of Education, The University of Georgia

Compass Point Books
Minneapolis, Minnesota

Compass Point Books
3722 West 50th Street, #115
Minneapolis, MN 55410

Visit Compass Point Books on the Internet at *www.compasspointbooks.com* or e-mail your
request to *custserv@compasspointbooks.com*

Photographs ©: Digital Stock, cover; Reuters/Gary Hershorn/Hulton Getty/Archive Photos, 4; Hulton
Getty/Archive Photos 6, 8; North Wind Picture Archives, 10, 14; Bettmann/Corbis 12; photographs by Franz
Jantzen, Collection of the Supreme Court of the United States, 16, 18; Corbis, 20.

Editors: E. Russell Primm, Emily J. Dolbear, Laura Driscoll, and Karen Commons
Photo Researchers: Svetlana Zhurkina and Jo Miller
Photo Selector: Linda S. Koutris
Designer: Melissa Voda

Library of Congress Cataloging-in-Publication Data
Murphy, Patricia J., 1963–
    The U.S. Supreme Court / by Patricia J. Murphy.
      p. cm. — (Let's see library)
    Includes bibliographical references and index.
    ISBN 0-7565-0197-0
    1. United States. Supreme Court—Juvenile literature. [1. United States. Supreme Court.] I. Title: United States
Supreme Court. II. Title. III. Let's see library. Our nation.
    KF8742.Z9 M85 2002
    347.73'26—dc21   2001004485

Table of Contents

What Is the U.S. Supreme Court?

The U.S. Supreme Court is the most important court in our country. Like all courts, the Supreme Court settles disagreements between two sides. These disagreements brought to court are called **cases**.

Many courts in the United States have only one judge. The U.S. Supreme Court has nine judges. Judges of the U.S. Supreme Court are called **justices**. Together, the justices listen to both sides. Then they decide in favor of one side. They also decide what our country's laws mean.

◄ *There are nine U.S. Supreme Court justices.*

How Was the Supreme Court Created?

In 1787, a group of Americans wrote the U.S. Constitution. A constitution is a written plan for how a government should work.

The writers of the U.S. Constitution decided the government should have three branches. One branch would make the laws. Another branch would make sure people follow the laws. A third branch would decide what the laws mean.

This third branch is called the **judicial branch**. All courts in the United States are part of this branch. The Supreme Court is the highest court of them all.

◄ *The U.S. Constitution was signed on September 17, 1787.*

What Does the Supreme Court Do?

The Supreme Court settles important cases. Other courts have often already given decisions. The Supreme Court will agree or disagree with those decisions. The Supreme Court's ruling in a case is final.

In some cases, the Supreme Court may decide that the law does not follow the U.S. Constitution. Then the Supreme Court can rule that it is no longer a law. For example, in 1954, the Supreme Court ruled that public schools couldn't educate whites and African-Americans separately.

◄ In 1957, National Guardsmen bring a black student to school in Arkansas. This was a result of the 1954 ruling that public schools couldn't teach whites and blacks separately.

How Does the Supreme Court Hear Cases?

Only important cases come to the Supreme Court. Four of the nine justices must agree to hear a case. Then the justices read papers from each side. The papers tell the justices more about the case.

Then, lawyers from each side have thirty minutes to speak in front of the justices. The justices listen and ask questions about the case.

◄ *A lawyer argues a case before the Supreme Court in 1910.*

How Does the Supreme Court Make Its Decisions?

After the justices hear a case in court, they meet in private. Then they vote. The justices often do not agree. When five justices agree, it becomes the Supreme Court's final decision.

For each case, one of the justices writes a paper. It gives the reasons why the Court made that decision. This paper is called the **majority opinion**. If a justice disagrees with this opinion, that justice can write his or her own opinion.

◄ *Justices talk together in the Supreme Court Building.*

Who Leads the Supreme Court?

The chief justice is the leader of the Supreme Court. The chief justice makes sure that the Supreme Court runs smoothly. He or she leads the Court's private meetings.

When voting, the chief justice has no more power than the other justices. He or she has one vote. When the chief justice agrees with the Court's decision in a case, he or she often writes the majority opinion. So far, only men have served as chief justice.

◄ *John Jay was the first chief justice of the Supreme Court.*

Where Does the Supreme Court Hear Cases?

The Supreme Court meets in the Supreme Court Building in Washington, D.C. Its courtroom has a long table. When the Supreme Court hears a case, the justices sit behind the table. The chief justice sits in the center. Behind the justices are four large columns and a red curtain.

The Supreme Court Building can hold up to 300 people. Some of the Supreme Court's meetings are open to the public.

◄ *The Supreme Court hears cases in this courtroom.*

When Does the Supreme Court Meet?

The Supreme Court hears cases from October to April. The Court usually hears cases several days a week. The justices write opinions for some cases immediately. But they write most opinions during May and June. From July through September, the Court takes a break.

Even when the Court is not hearing cases, the justices are busy. They study cases. They write about cases. They also think about which cases to hear in the future.

◄ *The justices meet in this room to discuss cases.*

How Does Someone Become a Justice?

The president of the United States chooses the Supreme Court justices. Presidents often pick justices who agree with their views. The U.S. Senate must approve the president's choices.

People chosen to be justices are usually judges or law professors. They do not have to be lawyers, however. Justices receive much respect for their knowledge and hard work.

Supreme Court justices often keep their jobs for life. They are justices until they die or choose to stop working.

◀ *In 1981, Sandra Day O'Connor became the first woman to serve as a Supreme Court justice.*

Glossary

cases—arguments brought to court

judicial branch—the part of the U.S. government that decides what laws mean

justices—judges of the U.S. Supreme Court

majority opinion—the written explanation of the Supreme Court's decision in a case

Did You Know?

• The words above the door of the Supreme Court Building are "Equal Justice Under Law." This means that everyone is treated the same.

• The first African-American member of the U.S. Supreme Court was Thurgood Marshall. President Lyndon Johnson chose him in 1967.

• When the Supreme Court is called to order, a crier says, "Oyez, oyez, oyez!" That means "Hear ye, hear ye, hear ye!"

Want to Know More?

At the Library

Aria, Barbara. *The Supreme Court.* New York: Franklin Watts, 1994.

Stein, R. Conrad. *Powers of the Supreme Court.* Chicago: Children's Press, 1995.

Summer, Lila, and Samuel G. Woods. *The Judiciary: Laws We Live By.* Austin, Tex.: Raintree Steck-Vaughn, 1993.

On the Web

Justice for Kids and Youth

http://www.usdoj.gov/kidspage/

For information about the judicial branch and the courts

Supreme Court of the United States

http://www.supremecourtus.gov

For the Supreme Court's calendar of meetings and a visitor's guide

Through the Mail

Supreme Court Public Information Officer

Supreme Court of the United States

Washington, DC 20543

To learn more about the Supreme Court

On the Road

Supreme Court Building

One First Street, N.E.

Washington, DC 20543

202/479-3030

To visit the Supreme Court in session

Index

About the Author

Patricia J. Murphy writes children's storybooks, nonfiction books, early readers, and poetry. She also writes for magazines, corporations, educational publishing companies, and museums. She is the owner of PattyCake Productions and lives in Northbrook, Illinois.